TULSA TIMES
A PICTORIAL HISTORY:
COMING OF AGE

Photographs From the Beryl D. Ford Collection
And the Tulsa World Archives

Text by Susan Everly-Douze
Edited by Terrell Lester

FOREWORD

"Tulsa Times: A Pictorial History" is a gathering of images of a city's rites of passage.

Volume III, "Coming of Age: 1942 to 1997," illustrates five decades of maturation: Tulsa emerging from a budding but still bumptious city into a metropolis.

The big picture focuses first on Tulsa's homefront effort during World War II. The conflict completed, the city turned its attention inward. The result was a boom economy that stretched the skyline upward and the city's boundaries outward, converting cow pasture to suburb. Tulsa wrestled with its legacy of "Oil Capital of the World," but made purposeful strides in aviation as a jet-age player – and in affairs maritime as the country's most inland port city.

These were the decades of progress, for dropping old-fashioned trappings. The interurban trolley made its last shuttle. The Ritz, the Orpheum, all the splendid downtown movie palaces, were razed. So was the Cimarron Ballroom. Progress also meant the city's first air-raid drills and community bomb shelters. Tulsa came to terms with the cold war.

For the camera's eye, new visions abounded: mothers manning B-24 bomber assembly lines and poodle-skirted teens bopping on "Dance Party," GI bungalows and Hudsons in the driveways, polio wards and evangelists' healing tents, fallout shelters and bootleggers' stills, drive-in eateries and hula hoops.

For this pictorial essay, the personal photographic archives of retired Tulsa World Chief Photographer Johnny Walker join the Beryl D. Ford Collection as the principal sources of photographs. Numerous other Tulsans and organizations also contributed.

Annotating a picture book of the city's past requires historical perspective and a grasp of municipal minutiae. Along with Tulsa historian Beryl D. Ford, retired Tulsa World Managing Editor Gene Curtis deserves gratitude for the sharing of both.

TABLE OF CONTENTS

Backing the Boys —————————————————————— 9

Going Up ———————————————————————————— 23

Spreading Out —————————————————————————— 41

Getting There ————————————————————————— 59

That's Entertainment ———————————————————— 83

Helping Out —————————————————————————— 111

The Way We Were ———————————————————————— 139

Coming Down ——————————————————————————— 175

New Directions —————————————————————————— 189

Bombers over Tulsa: a B-24 soared over the city of its crafting in 1943.

8

BACKING THE BOYS

"There's a war on, don't you know?" Uttered with grimace or grin, it was the catchall that explained the changes, prosaic and profound, wrought by World War II.

Gold stars hung in the parlor windows of grieving mothers, while other Tulsans danced away the wee hours at nightspots called the Music Box and Blue Moon. There were jobs for everybody, but countless autos were tireless. Matches, meat and candy bars also were in short supply, but bootlegged booze never flowed so freely. Housewives stayed home to stitch blackout shades, but Rosie the Riveter, by the hundreds, topped off her night shift by joining the crowd downtown at the midnight movie.

Even the zoo went to war. Gasoline rationing curtailed weekend out-of-town jaunts, and the zoo entertained huge crowds. Only four employees were left to tend 400 creatures. What's more, there were rattlesnakes to be milked for serum for soldiers and free lunches to find. Before the war, old horses routinely were donated to the zoo, but gasoline-short farmers were taking second looks at their nags and saving them for plowing.

The overseas conflict, however, proved a bracing tonic for Tulsa's economy. When the War Department awarded the city the $15 million Douglas Aircraft bomber plant, the shiny B-24 and B-26 bombers meant thousands of new jobs.

In addition, Tulsa's petroleum-related manu-facturing industry was ideal to retool for armaments. By the war's peak, 23,000 Tulsans had defense jobs.

Patriotism, however, meant more than an eight-hour shift at the bomber plant. Some 20,000 Tulsans volunteered for civil-defense work, bandage-making, war-bond selling, assisting the man-short fire department and meeting troop trains with cookies and coffee. Matrons donated jewelry. High-school boys trained as messengers, learning the location of every neighborhood clothesline so that they would not be decapitated running a blackout mission. Grandmothers signed up as "storytellers."

Every block had an air-raid warden, including one zealous neighborhood chief who proclaimed: "Every house is canvassed. We know not only where every cat and dog lives, but also that there is an average of 100 feet of water hose at every house."

Ultimately, the war touched every family. Almost 250,000 Oklahomans served. More than 700 Tulsans perished. When the fighting was over, many a Rosie the Riveter wasn't ready to give up her new freedom and paycheck. Many rural Oklahomans who had streamed into Tulsa to man the bomber plant weren't about to go back to the farm. Most importantly, thousands of young GIs, duty done, returned home with vast expectations. The city's fabric was forever changed.

A mile long and windowless, Douglas Aircraft's $15 million defense plant opened in Tulsa in July 1942 to manufacture B-24 and B-26 bombers.

The new bombers rolling off the assembly line translated into thousands of jobs for Oklahomans still stung by the Depression.

Even time clocks worked overtime. Oklahomans poured in from the countryside to fill shifts that kept the Douglas plant humming round the clock.

11

Taking time out from the assembly line for a sandwich and a suntan.

12

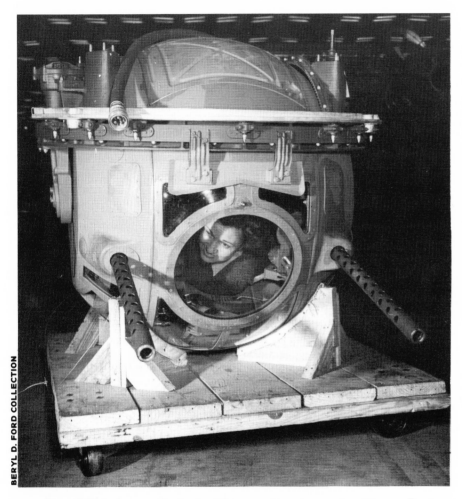

One of Tulsa's own Rosie the Riveters, Douglas worker Norma Baxter squeezed into the ball turret of a B-24 for a belly gunner's point of view.

Out of the house and onto the runway, war-plant work made women in pants and on the job a common sight.

13

The all-out war effort did not exclude the handicapped. At Douglas, 75 hearing-impaired Oklahomans tackled the bombers' complex electrical systems. Bright yellow arm bands protected the workers from accidents on the busy plant floor.

14

War planes were so vital that nothing, not even important design modifications, halted the assembly line. Instead, new bombers waited in line at a special modifications facility for last-minute changes. After the war, American Airlines leased the buildings for a maintenance depot.

15

Saluting a job well done, Douglas employees bid farewell to the "Tulsamerican," the last B-24 to roll off the Tulsa assembly line, August 1944.

16

PASSOVER SEDER FOR SOLDIERS OF CAMP GRUBER, OKLA. APRIL 19, 1943.

THE HOWARDS PHOTO. SINCE 1943

MUNICIPAL AUDITORIUM. MUSKOGEE, OKLA

Camp Gruber, near Muskogee, was a way station for soldiers from across the nation. In April 1943, Tulsa's Jewish community hosted a Passover Seder at Muskogee's municipal auditorium.

By 1942, almost 20,000 Tulsans had signed up for home-front work. Red Cross motor corps volunteer drivers posed with white-capped ladies from the Night Canteen Corps who kept the USO canteen in the Akdar Theater supplied with coffee, sandwiches and cookies. Career women who held full-time jobs made up the roster of the Night Canteen Corps.

The Canteen Corps not only kept the coffee urns hot but also met troop trains passing through Tulsa. The snacks they distributed were prepared in the demonstration kitchens of Public Service Co. and Oklahoma Natural Gas Co. The "canteen girls" also traveled by the busload to Camp Gruber to dance with the GIs.

18

They were "the women they left behind," but their hands weren't idle. In three years, Tulsa Red Cross volunteers prepared 230,000 surgical dressings for overseas hospitals.

Ration stamps were needed to buy a variety of goods, from sugar to gasoline.

From advertising bond drives to take-the-bus exhortations, patriotic billboards kept the war effort only a glance away.

19

The war still raged abroad, but Tulsans already had a temporary memorial in Boulder Park to honor the city's perished sons. Ultimately, more than 700 Tulsans would die in World War II. The homey monument was razed to make way in 1954 for a permanent memorial.

20

"TULSA ATTACKS!"

OFFICIAL
EIGHTH SERVICE COMMAND

WAR SHOW

SKELLY STADIUM

Saturday Evening, June 24, 1944

GATES OPEN 8 P. M.   OFFICIAL OPENING 9:30 P. M.

TREMENDOUS, DRAMATIC, THRILLING
BATTLE ACTION!!

1000 Combat Troops, Simulated Air Bombing Attacks, Tanks, Flame
Throwers, Bazookas, Tank & Anti-Air Craft Guns, Famous War Heroes

ADMIT ONE
COMPLIMENTARY   NO CHARGE   TAX
                      THIS TICKET MUST NOT BE SOLD   EXEMPT

SEC. I - EAST

ENTER GATE 6

GOOD ONLY
Saturday Evening, June 24, 1944

PUBLIC ADMITTED WITHOUT TICKETS
AFTER 9 P. M.

Children Not Admitted Unless
Accompanied By Parents

Patriotic extravaganzas, particularly mock battles, kept morale high and sold war bonds. On one occasion, Skelly Stadium was transformed into a Pacific battleground complete with palm trees and Japanese tanks. A 1943 rally featured Rudy Vallee singing the official Coast Guard song to a crowd of 5,000.

A new generation of "sidewalk superintendents" checked out the excavation for the new First National Bank Building, Fifth Street and Boston Avenue. Groundbreaking in 1948 celebrated Tulsa's first skyscraper since the start of the Depression.

22

GOING UP

The Great Depression was history. So was World War II.

For the first time in 20 years, the universal belief was that good times, finally, were here. Tulsans were ready to plan for tomorrow.

It was time to catch up. A time to shop, to buy tires, to get on a waiting list for a new automobile. But most of all, for scores, it was time to start a family, buy a bungalow, maybe start a mom-and-pop business.

For the rich, however, the confidence translated more boldly to the bricks and mortar of skyscrapers. Office space suddenly was in short supply. The city's skyline again burst upward in a building boom that would span the '50s.

Fittingly, First National Bank, Tulsa's oldest financial institution, kicked off the expansion in 1948 with downtown's first skyscraper since the Depression. Every square foot was leased two months before completion.

In 1950, on its 55th anniversary, the bank moved into the new headquarters. Designed by the architects of New York City's Rockefeller Center, the 20-story, glass and marble tower was headlined in "Life" magazine as a prototype of modern construction. Reassuringly, the new-fangled structure was dedicated to the tunes of the local swing bands of Johnnie Lee Wills and Leon McAuliffe.

The construction frenzy also triggered a fitful start for Tulsa's long-awaited civic center. A municipal pipe dream since the early '40s, razzle-dazzle preliminary concepts for the complex ranged from an Indian village to a working derrick complete with bottles of oil to sell to tourists. Clearing the six-block site, just to the west of the business district, was the first whole-sale bulldozing of the city's heritage, a mini neighborhood of the modest first homes of some of Tulsa's prominent pioneer families.

Ultimately, however, the ambitious plans yielded only a new county courthouse during those prosperous '50s. The city, a metropolis of 260,000, woefully needed a new city hall, a central library and an assembly center. But relief would be a decade away. Tulsans simply were too busy attending to business — their own business while times were good.

As a result, what the skyline of the "Oil Capital of the World" lacked in municipal magnificence, it made up for with striking new edifices from its namesake industry. Throughout the mid-'50s, the skyline was punctuated anew with the logos of Sunray Oil, Warren Petroleum, Amerada and Skelly Oil.

Tulsa, indeed, was a boom town anew. As one newspaper writer summed it up at the 1954 dedication of the $3.5 million Sunray building: "In a city like Tulsa ... new buildings are as commonplace as sunshine."

Rationing was only a wartime memory as prosperous Tulsans queued up for a glimpse of the latest in baubles, bangles and beads at Boswell's new jewelry shop, 509 S. Main St., in the Oil Capital Building. Boswell's old home, at Fifth Street and Boston Avenue, was razed to make way for the First National Bank Building.

Tulsa in 1948: the dual throttling of the Depression and World War II had left Tulsa's skyline virtually unchanged for 20 years. A building boom that spanned the '50s would change all that.

25

Dedicated July 29, 1950, the new glass and marble home of First National Bank, descendant of pioneer Tulsa's first bank, kicked off the prosperous '50s by giving the city its newest skyscraper. Tulsa historian and field construction engineer Beryl D. Ford posed during construction of the 20-story building at Fifth Street and Boston Avenue.

26

Downtown Tulsa in 1955.

Going up: the Enterprise Building, Sixth Street and Boston Avenue, *right*, in 1954, and J.C. Penney, Third and Main streets, *below*, in 1958.

Back in business for the boom: Virtually vacant between 1933 and 1944, the Genet Building, 910 S. Boston Ave., *far right*, was remodeled for much-needed office space. Known as the American Airlines Building, it housed the expanding airline's accounting department and, more memorably for the city's young bachelors, the stewardess school. Built in 1928 as a furniture store, the Art Deco-styled landmark, demolished in 1969, was one of Tulsa's last skyscrapers erected before the Depression.

Ronald Reagan, starring in "John Loves Mary," drew Tulsans to the Ritz theater, 18 W. Fourth St., in 1949 for a light-hearted aside to World War II.

Energy giants boosted Tulsa's claim to "Oil Capital of the World" with a spate of new buildings flashing their company logos onto the skyline. Sunray Oil Corp. dedicated its 12-story office building, 907 S. Detroit Ave., *right*, in October 1954, complete with the top floor renumbered pseudo 13 for luck. In 1956, Warren Petroleum Corp., *above*, moved to the then-residential neighborhood of Boulder Avenue at 13th Street. Amerada Petroleum Corp., *upper left*, in 1958 was taking over the corner of Sixth Street and Denver Avenue.

30

Abandoned streetcar tracks at Archer Street and Denver Avenue were mute testimony that in 1956 the auto was king of the road.

By the mid-'50s, a scarcity of downtown parking spaces made banking on the go the way to pay. In January 1955, the National Bank of Tulsa opened a motor bank on the northwest corner of Fourth Street and Cincinnati Avenue.

31

The piemen of Route 66: Bama Pie was a family affair in 1942 operating from a frame building at 11th Street and Delaware Avenue. By 1953, business boomed at 25,000 pies a day and the baking facilities had begun to fill the block.

The war's end prompted an explosion of new small businesses that would become familiar community signposts. Less than a year after Germany surrendered, Farmers and Merchants State Bank, today F&M Bank and Trust Co., opened in a small storefront at 1114 S. Harvard Ave, *top right*. The fledgling Moody's Jewelry, *upper left*, briefly was its neighbor at 1130 S. Harvard Ave. In the fall of 1946, founder Ernest Moody, *left*, moved his store, *above*, across the street. This time he was to share a building with Steve's Sundry. Owner Steve Stephenson trained as a manager for the dime-store chain S.H. Kress, but after a wartime stint in the Navy decided on a business of his own. He opened shop in 1947.

34 Tulsa in 1957 from 15th Street looking north between Boulder Avenue and Main Street. The Skelly Building
    would be completed a year later.

Getting your winks on Route 66: Whitts Motel, 5318 E. 11th St., was a landmark rest stop on the fabled highway during the '40s and '50s.

The Ambassador Hotel, 7 W. 14th St., built in 1928, retained its status in the late '40s as one of Tulsa's premier residences. The apartments were favored by oilmen and their families.

In the mid-'50s, the quarter-century-old Mayo Hotel still dominated the Cheyenne Avenue scene.

In the '40s, the list of residents at the Sophian Plaza, 1500 S. Frisco Ave., one of the city's first high-rise apartment houses, read like a who's who of social and business circles.

The late '50s was downtown Tulsa's last hurrah as *the* place to shop and congregate. The soda fountain at
Walgreens, Fourth and Main streets, was a popular gathering spot.

A decade of postwar construction complete, Tulsa closed out the '50s with a sparkling new profile.

The streets were freshly paved but dusty, the GI bungalows were spanking new — and a "giant hamburger" cost a quarter. It was the early '50s and the Brookside boom led and typified Tulsa's postwar suburban push. The ribbon-like neighborhood that stretched along Peoria Avenue from 31st to 51st streets found its epicenter at 38th Place and Peoria.

40

SPREADING OUT

Home from the beaches of Normandy, the islands of the Pacific, a generation of Tulsans was ready for a permanent beachhead, this time in its own hometown.

The veterans and their families cast their sights beyond downtown's concrete canyons, beyond the tree-lined streets where oil money had built mansions. They looked instead to the pasture-studded horizons, just beyond the city limits.

What they found were new bungalows, dream houses for as little as $7,000. Less than $300 down made many ex-GIs homeowners.

By the late '40s, punctuated by rows of these cookie-cutter "GI houses," Tulsa's push to a suburban profile was on. Nothing epitomized the phenomenon better than the overnight development of Brookside, a once-sleepy community flanking Peoria Avenue. Before construction dust had settled, developers were luring would-be homesteaders, and merchants were promoting a casual alternative to downtown's white-gloved shopping. And, Brookside was just the beginning.

Intensified by an already acute housing shortage, a legacy of the war years, the '50s was the new decade to strike it rich. This time, however, fortunes were made in real estate — not just in homes but in what would be the natural complement to suburbia, the shopping center.

The 1952 opening of Utica Square, once a countryside golf driving range, kicked off the contest with downtown merchants for customers.

The same year, refinery worker-turned-builder Vernon L. Mudd, who had modeled much of Brookside, took another pioneer plunge with Bellaire Village, a block-long center on Peoria Avenue at 51st Street. Predictably, it was criticized as too far out in the country.

The mid-'50s brought a quick cloning of the center concept. Ranch Acres was dubbed swank with its pink stone frontage. East Tulsa boasted Mayo Meadows with its "California contemporary" motif. By 1956, downtown shops began to hurt; two years later, Sears, Roebuck and Co., a retail mainstay, deserted for 21st Street and Yale Avenue. A decade later, downtown's fate as a has-been shopping mecca was all but sealed with the opening of the giant shopping complexes of Southland and Southroads.

Tulsa's epicenter no longer was Fourth and Main streets. It was on the move, but the direction decidedly was south and east. Tulsa pioneer W.L. North figured that out in 1956 when Mudd, who became the first major developer of South Tulsa, bought 100 acres of North's farmland, near Harvard Avenue and 51st Street, to expand his Woodland Acres addition. North, 90 at the time of the transaction, reminisced about his once-rural homestead purchased in 1904 and dubbed "Lou North's Corner" by travellers.

Once, a buggy trip to town took a half day. "Now," said North, who had watched the city grow up around him, "I'm right in Tulsa."

41

A college degree was top priority for thousands of GIs returning from World War II, and enrollment at the University of Tulsa increased fivefold from 1943 to 1949. Barracks from Camp Gruber were rushed in for classrooms and student housing. A nearby church doubled as a lecture hall. In 1952, the new Mabee dormitories and Lorton Hall in the foreground and the barracks in the rear epitomized the expansion.

42

Above: All too familiar: hundreds of TU soldiers-turned-scholars discovered their campus quarters were old Army barracks. The housing was dubbed "Vets' Village." *Left*: By the late '40s, young veterans predominated at TU.

The price was right, and the cookie-cutter bungalows, *below*, aimed at the GI market in the early '50s became synonymous with Brookside. A particularly hot seller was a no-frills complex off Peoria Avenue at 38th Place, *right*, with identical units that stretched for blocks.

Brookside's main street, Peoria Avenue, looking north from 33rd Street in 1951.

44

In 1952, Peoria Avenue at 41st Street, *top*, had the look of a country road, but postwar housing additions, *bottom*, were fast changing the landscape.

45

Downtown was the place to shop and dressed to the nines was the way to go. That was a Tulsa tradition. In 1951, Brookside merchants challenged the white-gloved garb and the concrete-canyon confines with the first Brookside Shorts Day. By 1957, Shorts Day was an entertainment extravaganza that ranged from big band sounds to apple bobbing. Downtown stores countered suburban wooing of customers with a billboard campaign.

Short shorts honed a competitive edge in the 1959 Miss Brookside contest.

47

Brookside landmarks: Pennington's Drive In, 4235 S. Peoria Ave., opened in 1951. Fried shrimp and blackbottom pie made the family-owned eatery a neighborhood tradition. The Brookside Market, 3620 S. Peoria Ave., touted fancy foodstuffs and home delivery. Roller-skating mania kept the Brookside Coliseum, 3730 S. Peoria Ave., gliding prosperously through the '50s, but by 1963 the rink was closed.

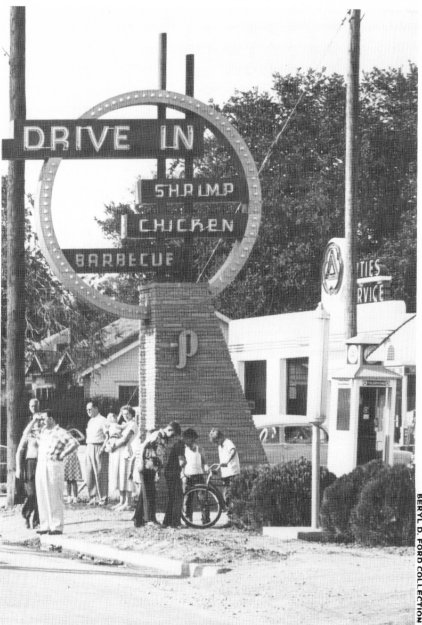

48

All the right stuff: A postwar dream house, circa 1955, in Boman Acres.

Pushing Tulsa's boundaries farther south, Southern Village opened model homes in 1954 at 61st Street and Yorktown Avenue. Touted as "mass produced deluxe residences," the houses ranged from $18,000 to $35,000.

Tract housing on North Garrison Avenue typified the '50s construction boom in North Tulsa, which boasted its own major shopping center, Northland, anchored by Brown-Dunkin and Froug's department stores.

Opened in May 1952 on a former golf driving range, Utica Square, Tulsa's first major suburban shopping center, was considered a gamble at the time, but quickly became downtown's first heavyweight competition for customers.

The intersection of 41st Street and Yale Avenue, looking east, was still out in the country in the early '60s, but the city was moving relentlessly south and east. Construction of Southland, dubbed Oklahoma's biggest and most modern shopping center, began in 1963 and was completed in 1965 with Brown-Dunkin and other traditional downtown retailers as tenants. Across 41st Street, Southroads Mall opened in 1967.

By 1967, the bustling intersection of 41st Street and Yale Avenue, home of the two new shopping centers, had permanently pushed the city's focal point away from downtown. The vast open space to the south and east was a magnet for developers.

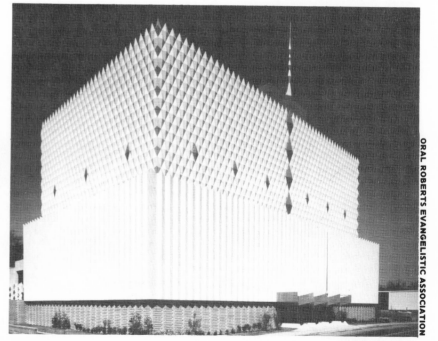

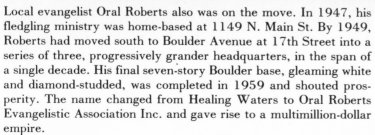

Local evangelist Oral Roberts also was on the move. In 1947, his fledgling ministry was home-based at 1149 N. Main St. By 1949, Roberts had moved south to Boulder Avenue at 17th Street into a series of three, progressively grander headquarters, in the span of a single decade. His final seven-story Boulder base, gleaming white and diamond-studded, was completed in 1959 and shouted prosperity. The name changed from Healing Waters to Oral Roberts Evangelistic Association Inc. and gave rise to a multimillion-dollar empire.

Thomas A. Edison junior and senior high school students did double shifts in the junior high building, 3000 E. 41st St., until the April 1957 completion of the high school. Because of the rapid growth of South Tulsa, the facility was deemed too small even before it was completed. Prefab classrooms provided a roof over students' heads during construction.

55

Prime real estate of the future: 41st Street and Sheridan Road in 1955.

Admiral Place and Sheridan Road was the focal point of late-'50s expansion in East Tulsa.

Looking north on Memorial Drive at 51st Street: still a country scene in the mid-'60s.

101 MILES

AMERICA'S MOST BEAUTIFUL CITY

The OIL CAPITAL of the WORLD

Visit Tulsa...See

9000 Plants in Bloom
SIX ACRES

America's Most Beautiful
ROSE
GARDEN
FREE ADMISSION

Knapp Adv. Co.

Going our way? That's what Tulsa businessmen had in mind in the mid-'50s when they sponsored a series of come-look-us-over highway billboards.

GETTING THERE

By land, by air, by waterway, Tulsa tackled its transportation priorities a decade at a time.

Gasoline and tire shortages were over. The city's boundaries were expanding. It was the '50s. Tulsa had asphalt on its mind.

At first, it seemed so simple. Bond issues passed. A grid pattern of new streets stretched into farmland. Tulsa became an enviable terminus of two ultra modern highways, the Turner Turnpike, dedicated in 1953, and four years later, the Will Rogers Turnpike.

Then came Skelly Drive, Tulsa's first multi-lane, limited access expressway — and cause of a decade-long municipal headache of political shenanigans, route disputes, lawsuits, interminable delays and charges of shoddy construction.

The roadway was a maze of contradictions. Some Tulsa planners wanted a bypass around the city; others wanted an expressway through the city. The bypass proponents won, initially, except the roadway, ultimately, became an expressway. Called the 51st Street Bypass, little of the route was on 51st Street. Property owners who expected to pocket a bundle selling right-of-way went to court; so did property owners who suddenly were dispossessed by the bypass. Ultimately, it became Interstate 44 — except it did not meet interstate standards and early portions had to be redone.

Finally, on Nov. 21, 1958, the Skelly Bypass opened. During the eight years it took to complete the mere 18 miles, some almost immediately crumbling, the Turner and Will Rogers turnpikes had been started and completed. What's more, the continuous controversy soured many a Tulsan for road projects to come. The badly needed Broken Arrow Expressway, repeatedly promised through the '50s, did not get broken ground until July 1960.

The '60s, however, did see Tulsa soar confidently into the jet age with the same acumen its pioneer oil barons showed in landing the city's first airport in 1928 with a studhorse note.

In June 1959, American Airlines dedicated a $20 million jet overhaul facility, the first of its kind. Tulsa, where aviation was second only to oil as its largest industry, was paying attention. Only a few months later, the city launched a $9.7 million airport modernization program for the '60s, including a new terminal. In 1963, Tulsa Municipal Airport became Tulsa International Airport and one of only seven municipal airports in the country with a runway long enough to handle the big jets.

Tulsa's ultimate transportation coup, navigation of the Arkansas River, was achieved in the '70s. The Port of Catoosa, opened in 1971, was the terminus in a 444-mile navigation system to the oceans of the world via the Arkansas, Verdigris and Mississippi rivers. Landlocked Tulsa had became the country's most inland waterport.

In 1955, cowboys still escorted hungry Texas steers to the lush bluestem pastures of northern Tulsa County for summer fattening.

Countless head of cattle passed through the pens of the Tulsa Stockyards during its 42-year tenure on the Sand Springs line. Despite critics' scoffs that you could not turn the nation's Oil Capital into a little Chicago, the yards, by the early '40s, had made Tulsa the livestock marketing center of eastern Oklahoma. Urbanization trimmed sales and the yard was closed December 1976.

TULSA WORLD, JOHNNY WALKER

TULSA STOCKYARDS-HOG & SHEEP DIVISION.

BARBER SHOP 25¢ 20¢

BERYL D. FORD COLLECTION

60

The Sand Springs Railway Co.'s interurban originally was built to transport workers from Tulsa to Charles Page's new industrial townsite of Sand Springs. For thousands of Tulsans, however, the trolley was synonymous with Sunday afternoon outings. The streetcars plied the tracks round the clock from 1911 until 1955.

61

For four decades, a slatted wood seat on the clattering "struggle buggies" remained 10 cents for adults, 5 cents for children. In 1952, the adult fare rose to 15 cents.

62

Left: Waiting to "ride the line."
Lower left: In Tulsa's interurban waiting room, Archer Street and Boston Avenue, everyone knew the schedule for the 30-minute ride to Sand Springs: trains every 20 minutes until 10:30 p.m. Then the "owl car" began its hourly runs.
Below: Oklahoma's trolley era ended in January 1955 when the Sand Springs interurban, believed to be the state's last trolley line, made its final run. Diesel buses replaced the streetcars.

Above: The last of the whistle-stop campaigners, David Hall, elected Oklahoma governor in 1970, took to the rails in 1966 for what was believed to be the final chapter of state politicking from a passenger train.

Right: In 1961, conventioneers chose the train.

Upper right: Train buffs bid farewell to passenger service for Tulsa in the mid-'60s.

Union Bus Terminal, Fourth Street and Cincinnati Avenue, was in low gear in 1946 following the war years when Tulsans' love affair with the automobile had been put on hold by gasoline rationing and tire shortages.

Donut-dunking regulars at landmark Uncle Willie's, First Street and Boston Avenue, got a bang with their sinkers in 1954 when a "skip the fuss" bus didn't.

A queue of cabs added to the Main Street bustle in 1946.

66

A Pontiac Silver Streak was one of 280 Yellow Cabs that cruised Tulsa streets in 1953. The company began in 1905 with horse-pulled buckboards but entered the auto age five years later with four Dodges.

Dispatching cabs in the '50s.

CARS OF THE TIMES

In 1953, the Tulsa gates to the Turner Turnpike, one of the nation's first long-distance toll roads, swung open to launch a new chapter in state transportation. The $38 million pioneer pike was a streamlined conduit between Tulsa and Oklahoma City. The speed limit originally was to have been 90 mph but was pulled back to 70 mph by opening day.

72

Upper left: In the mid-'50s, the two-laning of the Okmulgee Beeline section of U.S. 75 was cause for a picnic celebration.

Left: Groundbreaking on July 29, 1960, for the long-awaited Broken Arrow Expressway.

Above: The Skelly Bypass, in 1956, cut a swath through the Lou North farm at 51st Street and Harvard Avenue.

Terrain around the Keystone Dam project was so rugged that mules bested machinery in some jobs. The dam was completed in 1964.

Construction of the Keystone Expressway spanned 1966 to 1973.

The still bulldozer-raw path of the Crosstown Expressway wound its way through East Tulsa in 1967. The overpass at Joplin Avenue and Admiral Place was under construction.

Overhauling an American Airlines DC-3 at Tulsa Municipal Airport in 1946.

Tulsa's stylish front door in the early '40s.

A row of gleaming Cadillac limousines in the mid-'50s complemented the Art Deco facade of Tulsa Municipal Airport. The terminal, built in 1932, would soon be victim of the jet age.

American AA Airlines

FLIGHTS OPERATING
WEDNESDAY
FROM TULSA

DESTINATION	FLIGHTS	DEPT. TIME
CHICAGO	2	9:32AM , 11:47 AM
DALLAS/ FT. WORTH	2	6:50 PM NON STOP , 9:13 PM
NEW YORK	2	
LOS ANGELES	1	
[SAN F]RANCISCO	2	
[WASH]INGTON DC	1	
[ST. L]OUIS	2	
[DET]ROIT	2	
[PHO]ENIX	1	
[OKLAHO]MA CITY	2	
[NASHVI]LLE	1	
[MILWAU]KEE	1	
[AKR]ON	1	
[DENVE]R	2	

Promoting a full-service airport: a 1957 Ford Fairlane 500 ready-to-rent met Braniff's twin-engine Convair. The aircraft was one of the new generation of passenger planes that would replace the diehard DC-3.

Penciling in the schedule in the late '50s.

WELCOME
FOLKS

It was the dawn of the jet age, but groundbreaking ceremonies for Tulsa International Airport, Nov. 4, 1959, had a folksy air. The terminal building itself was dedicated Nov. 16, 1961, but portable stoplights directed runway traffic throughout expansion construction.

Introducing Tulsa to the waterways of the world, the Arkansas River Navigation System and its terminus, the Port of Catoosa, opened Dec. 31, 1970. The first commercial barge to travel the entire 444-mile length of the McClellan-Kerr Navigation System arrived at Tulsa's new port Jan. 21, 1971, carrying 650 tons of newsprint. The port's turning basin was the end of the line for the McClellan-Kerr Navigation System.

81

When "The Lawton Story: The Prince of Peace" premiered in that southwestern Oklahoma city in 1949, seats priced at $1,000 were the highest in movie history. The $2.5 million filming of the Lawton Easter pageant in the Wichita Mountains was the first full-length sound and color movie of the life of Christ. Tulsa audiences caught the movie at the Plaza Theater, 15th Street and Peoria Avenue.

THAT'S ENTERTAINMENT

The more the merrier. That was Tulsa's crowd credo when it came to having a good time.

In pioneer days, rag-tag bands had 'em lined up, toe-tappin' on Main Street. A Wild West show, teetotalers' crusade, or returning GIs all merited parades. Crowds spilled onto the streets surrounding Cain's Ballroom for an earful of Texas Playboy tunes. They were back in force to catch Strangler Lewis wrestling at the Coliseum, soldiers staging a mock Pacific battle at a palm-strewn Skelly Stadium, or adventuresome young ladies posing in the abbreviated dress that made Brookside Shorts Day.

At the century's turn, the lure of professional baseball had the whole town pouring into the bleachers. This love affair continued to flourish, and the Tulsa Oilers' attendance peaked during the late '40s and '50s.

All these crowds, however, were decidedly minor league compared with the events of April 13, 1949. Tulsa topped its own best acts, past and, almost assuredly, future. More than 100,000 exuburant fans descended on downtown for "Tulsa Day," a celebration of the world premiere of the movie "Tulsa." They were treated to a five-mile-long parade featuring not only Hollywood stars, but also every type of petroleum paraphernalia that could be put on wheels.

That night, "Tulsa," a depiction of the city's oil boom days that gave new meaning to melodrama, opened simultaneously at the big four downtown theaters, the Ritz, Orpheum, Rialto and Majestic. Despite a full day of festivities, good-timing Tulsans queued in block-long lines for the distinction of being first-nighters.

They only were doing what came naturally. Since the first dime thriller flickered mutely across the Lyric Theater screen, Tulsa had been a movie-going town. In its heyday, the city claimed 29 "hardtop" cinemas with names like Dreamland, Cameo, Gayety and Star.

From a big date in the balcony to every kid's ideal, the 10-cent Saturday matinee, entertainment just couldn't get any better than sitting en masse in front of the big silver screen. It couldn't, that is, until the fall of 1949.

Suddenly that silent camraderie, not to mention the roaring ballpark crowd and the pulsating ballroom dance floors, had competition.

Television was coming to Tulsa.

"Arthur Godfrey and Friends;" "Toast of the Town" with Ed Sullivan; Howdy Doody; Kukla, Fran and Ollie. Soon they would all be at Tulsans' finger tips — without ever leaving home.

It was, promoters proclaimed, "a new wonderland of sight and sound, overcoming the barriers of distance and darkness to bring the world right into your living room."

Engineers threw the switch Nov. 30, 1949. Some Tulsans, however, couldn't wait. They stayed home and plugged in a whole month earlier — just to watch the test-pattern squiggles.

More than 100,000 people turned out April 13, 1949, for what was undoubtedly the Oil Capital's biggest, most enthusiastic civic party ever, a celebratory extravaganza for the world premiere of the movie "Tulsa." Highlighting the gala, proclaimed "Tulsa Day" by the governor, was a five-mile-long parade displaying an only-in-Tulsa melange of Hollywood stars, including Susan Hayward, Robert Preston and Chill Wills, and a dizzying array of oil industry equipment, led by a float carrying a complete, "modern" filling station.

84

Susan Hayward, who later square-danced on Tulsa's streets, was the parade's chief attraction. In the film, a Hollywood melodrama of Tulsa's oil boom days, she played Cherokee Lansing, a rancher's daughter — "half angel, half wildcat ... All Woman."

Children were excused from school; oil companies closed their offices. The resulting crowd spilled uncontrollably into the street, almost mobbing the Hollywood luminaries. The trial of a bigtime bootlegger had to be postponed that day because none of the arresting officers appeared in court. They were busy guarding Miss Hayward.

The world's largest portable drilling rig was set up at Fourth and Main streets as a pedestal for Miss Hayward.

A rooftop parade perch was the closest that some Tulsans could get to the Hollywood stars. "Tulsa" opened simultaneously in four downtown theaters, the Ritz, Orpheum, Rialto and Majestic, but crowds of would-be first-nighters still were turned away. What they missed, according to movie advertising, was a technicolor tale of "... a city of red-blooded men of adventure ... and the tempestuous woman who sought to rule. A seething cauldron of emotion that boiled over and burst into flame at the whisper of a single word ... oil!"

The Ritz, 18 W. Fourth St., was Tulsa's ultimate motion picture theater and met with the most dignified end. Unlike the other major downtown theaters that settled for "B" movies, the Ritz remained a first-run house until it closed in 1960. The Tower, 1105 S. Denver Ave., dubbed "Tulsa's finest suburban theater" when it was constructed in 1937, specialized in foreign films after World War II. In the '50s, evangelist Billy Hargis held revivals there. The Majestic, 406 S. Main St., screened Tulsa's first talkie and still was a premier theater in 1947 and into the '60s. It was an X-rated movie house when it was demolished in 1973.

HOWARD HOPKINS PHOTOGRAPHY

The Tulsa, 215 S. Main St., in the early '50s.

BERYL D. FORD COLLECTION

Boasting the best balcony of any Tulsa movie theater, the Delman, built at 15th Street and Lewis Avenue in the mid-'30s, still was a gleaming, modernistic beacon in 1949.

Ten cents for the movie and a nickel each for popcorn, Milk Duds and a Coke added up to a perfect Saturday afternoon's entertainment in the mid-'50s at the Uptown and Cozy theaters on the Main Street viaduct.

90

One of Tulsa's favorite eateries in the '40s and '50s was Frank's Pig Stand, 15th Street and Boston Avenue.

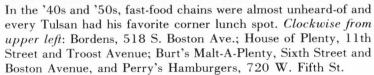

In the '40s and '50s, fast-food chains were almost unheard-of and every Tulsan had his favorite corner lunch spot. *Clockwise from upper left*: Bordens, 518 S. Boston Ave.; House of Plenty, 11th Street and Troost Avenue; Burt's Malt-A-Plenty, Sixth Street and Boston Avenue, and Perry's Hamburgers, 720 W. Fifth St.

From the corner jukebox to the white-capped soda jerks, Burt's Good Humor Ice Cream Store, 16 E. 18th St., was the classic ice cream parlor. Harry B. Burt, the owner, invented ice cream on a stick.

Hawk Dairy, 11th Street and Lewis Avenue, before its 1948 expansion. Many a date ended at Hawk's soda fountain.

94

Wynn's Cafe, Admiral Place and Harvard Avenue, in the late '40s.

The '50s and '60s were synonymous with drive-ins. Described as Tulsa's "first swanky drive-in," Norman Angel's Auto Cafe, Admiral Place and Memorial Drive, had room for 90 cars and catered to adults. Barney's Hub, 11th Street and Boulder Avenue, was the eatery of choice for Central High School students.

The Louisiane, 118 E. 18th St., and the Italian Inn, 1604 S. Main St., were Tulsa traditions in fine dining. But arguably Tulsa's most fondly remembered restaurant was Bishop's, 510 S. Main St. The 24-hour landmark eatery was demolished for a parking lot in February 1966 after more than 35 years at its Main Street location. The parking lot later gave way to State Federal Savings and Loan.

97

Honey Hudgen and her combo was the act of choice at Western Village, Tulsa's swank forerunner of today's fancy highway hostelries. From the late '40s until the early '60s, Miss Hudgen was Tulsa's official, but unpaid, hostess counted on by the Chamber of Commerce to charm visiting dignitaries.

Built in 1952 on heavily traveled Admiral Place, a shortcut from downtown Tulsa to U.S. 66, Western Village in its '50s heyday boasted resort-like facilities including 97 rooms and suites, landing strip, kidney-shaped pool with cabanas, 18-hole golf course and gourmet restaurant.

99

Municipal tennis courts became al
fresco ballrooms in 1954 as Tulsans
do-si-doed under the stars.

Traditional brush
arbors again were
erected in 1962 as
a shady backdrop
for spectators en-
joying a squaw
dance at an Indian
powwow.

Always a baseball town, Tulsa had a professional team two years before Oklahoma achieved statehood. In 1934, old McNulty Park, Tenth Street and Elgin Avenue, was replaced by Oiler Park, 15th Street and Sandusky Avenue. The wooden structure was home to such popular stars as Russ Burns, Joe "Speedo" Patterson and Walt "No Neck" Williams.

The popularity of professional baseball exploded after World War II, setting attendance records. In 1956, the Tulsa Oilers, who played in the Texas League, drew 153,612 fans.

101

Originally built to bring professional hockey to Tulsa, Sam Avey's Coliseum, Fifth Street and Elgin Avenue, was the city's largest auditorium and most beloved sports palace.

102

Saturday night, Sept. 20, 1952, was the Coliseum's grand finale. Lightning struck and set off the biggest fire in the city's history. Some 150 firemen fought the wind-whipped blaze, but all in vain. More than 12,000 Tulsans watched, recalling the hockey and basketball games, political conventions, boxing bouts, family skating, piano concerts, and much, much more. Sam Avey, owner and longtime sports promoter, left before the flames were squelched. "I've had too many happy memories in that old barn," he said, "to want to watch it die."

It was the end of an era. The Coliseum was reduced to a pile of twisted steel, ashes and stone. The next day, thousands viewed the rubble; many wept. Besides the emotional loss, Tulsa was left without an adequate auditorium.

103

Leon McAuliffe, left, along with Bob Wills, center, and Johnnie Lee Wills, made Tulsa synonymous with western swing. The trio in 1957.

Tulsa's beautiful white elephant, the Akdar Theater, Fourth Street and Denver Avenue, saw multiple reincarnations from opera house to wrestling arena before its 1973 demolition. In 1953, the hall became Leon McAuliffe's popular Cimarron Ballroom.

Even as a '50s ballroom, the Akdar-turned-Cimarron retained its '20s elegance.

105

A veteran of dance halls and radio, Leon McAuliffe adapted his western swing to Tulsa's newest entertainment medium, television. McAuliffe, performing in the early '60s, was on KOTV's entertainment roster Nov. 30, 1949, the day commercial television came to Tulsa.

KOTV's early-day programming ran from 6 p.m. to 10:30 p.m. The station boasted the largest television studio in the country, 112 feet long, 60 feet wide and 20 feet high.

In 1964, Dance Party made Tulsa teens stars for a day. Tulsans who owed their continued fame to the little black box included Spanky McFarland of "Our Gang," Patti Page and Anita Bryant.

The combo at practice included Gerald Westby on the piano, Jack Freese on the drums and Johnson Hill Jr. on the banjo.

It was a rare treat indeed, a performance by the "Rare Bach and Let 'em Have It Boys." The irrepressible combo of local businessmen-philanthropists let loose with its self-styled Dixieland repertoire for charity events. The performances were once described as combining Louis Armstrong and Harpo Marx. Favorites included "Minuet in G-Whiz," "Breathless Schottische from Schmirnoff," and "Show Me a Home Where the Buffalo Roam and I'll Show You a House That's a Mess."

Bagging for Brookside: Tulsans united in 1957 to turn back the encroaching Arkansas River.

HELPING OUT

Tulsa was a town that took care of its own.

Rallying for a "smash polio" campaign or a downtown beautification drive came naturally. So did mothers marching for safer school crossings or a mayor leading a Red Cross blood drive by personal example.

Nothing, however, so much inspired a collective helping hand as the threat of the moody Arkansas River roiling over its banks. Over the decades, would-be good Samaritans got plenty of practice. Flooding, particularly before levees fettered the flow, was as predictable as spring rains.

Despite sandbagging efforts, the flood of 1923 left 4,000 people in West Tulsa and Sand Springs homeless. By the '40s, Civil Defense and Red Cross volunteers had honed their rescue-relief tasks to a science. When spring clouds banked up, rescue-boat motors were primed and shelters readied. Predictably, it would be another night of navigating the Sand Springs line picking up hapless victims.

This spirit of volunteerism rose to new heights in 1957 when the Arkansas raged once more. This time, the river had a toothsome new target. Brookside, once a small neighborhood, had exploded with development after World War II. GI housing spread block after block virtually down to the river's edge.

Forecasters were predicting record waters. Almost 2,000 families headed for higher ground. Hundreds of volunteers turned out to help.

More than 64,000 sandbags were filled to form levees to hold back the swelling river. As the water climbed, this makeshift engineering became more creative. At least one junked auto was packed with sandbags and lowered into the river to stop the flow to a flooded creek.

The rally against the Arkansas did not stop at the levees. Volunteers visited each flood-prone residence to offer assistance. Trucks were recruited for free moving service. Churches, schools and private homes were transformed into shelters and canteens. Hundreds more volunteers manned the shelters, baby-sat and cooked hot meals for the sandbaggers and flood refugees.

The river backed up into storm sewers flooding streets and yards. Brookside resembled a lake dotted with house islands. The water dampened garages and basements, but most houses remained dry. Along Riverside Drive, the river broke over the sandbagged levee in only one block.

The flood, it seemed, never matched forecasters' dire predictions. What did rise to everyone's expectations, and more, was Tulsa's helping hand.

Bunting, a band and patriotic messages drew a Main Street crowd in 1949.

Tulsans have always loved a parade, and the American Legion obliged in 1949 with a postwar procession up Boston Avenue.

Memories of loved ones lost to World War II and the Korean War still were fresh in 1957 as Tulsans gathered at the Boulder Park Memorial to Veterans of Foreign Wars.

A 1954 open house at City Hall, Fourth Street and Cincinnati Avenue, called for a parade of Tulsa's fire-fighting apparatus.

Mayor James Maxwell, at head of table, was a 31-year-old florist and political unknown in 1958 when he became the city's youngest chief executive and directed the city council.

116

Mayor James Maxwell, one of only three men to head the city for four terms, led by personal example as well. A billboard in front of the County Courthouse, Sixth Street and Boulder Avenue, pictured the mayor donating blood to the Tulsa Red Cross.

Getting out the vote was top priority in 1956 as Tulsans were courted with mobile registration trailers and some pint-size politicians.

Down and definitely out, this evicted family in the mid-'60s had its belongings piled at the curb for non-payment of rent.

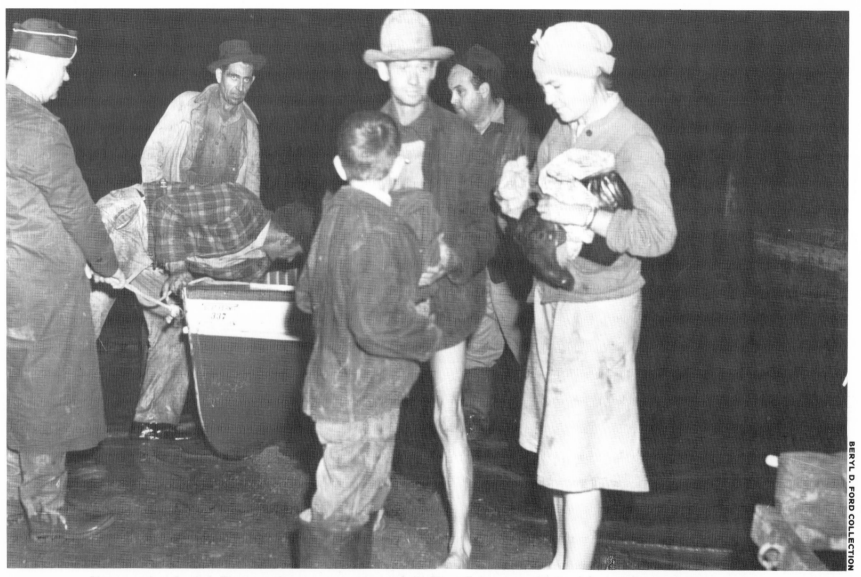

If it poured, it flooded. That was the conventional wisdom in West Tulsa along the Sand Springs line in the '40s before levees were constructed to rein in the Arkansas River. Civil Defense workers evacuated families by boat. Tulsa Red Cross volunteers provided shelter, food and occasional delousing at the Sixth Street Armory.

Evacuation work complete, Civil Defense workers in the early '40s posed with their rescue fleet at a flooded market at 3215 Charles Page Blvd. Inside, a handshake for a job well done.

Fully developed to Riverside Drive, the subdivisions of Brookside got their first serious taste of the mighty Arkansas River with the flood of 1957.

122

Flood waters on Riverside Drive rose toward the Midland Valley bridge as volunteers fought back.

123

Some 4,000 Brooksiders headed to higher ground.

A junked auto, loaded with sandbags, was lowered into the mouth of a flooded creek near 33rd Street at Riverside Drive.

High and dry but forlorn, man's best friend waited atop his doghouse for flood waters to recede.

It was touch and go for sandbaggers. Terra firma dwindled and the Arkansas and its backwater moved closer.

Tulsans proved their mettle when they turned out by the hundreds to fill sandbags and build levees.

A community affair: while some Tulsans constructed makeshift levees, others volunteered to house evacuees, move furniture, babysit and cook flapjack breakfasts for flood workers.

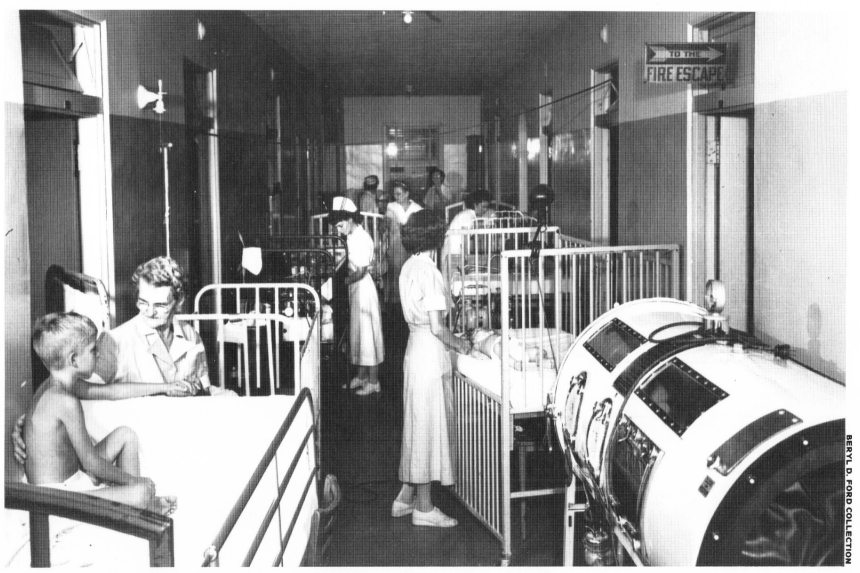

Parents lived in fear, and many kept their youngsters out of movie theaters and public swimming pools in the late '40s and early '50s when polio ravaged the nation. In Tulsa, the peak of the epidemic was in 1952. Polio wards at Hillcrest Hospital were so full that beds with stricken youngsters lined the corridors.

128

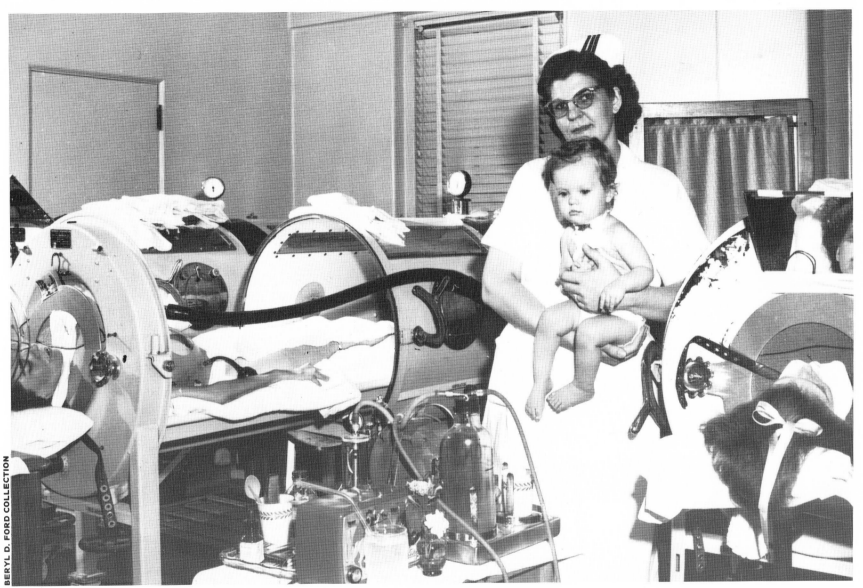

Iron lungs, the lifeline for paralyzed breathing muscles, most resembled a casket, and many victims took their last breaths inside the metal cocoons. Nurses tending the ailing children often worked round the clock because their co-workers who had young children were relieved of ward duty.

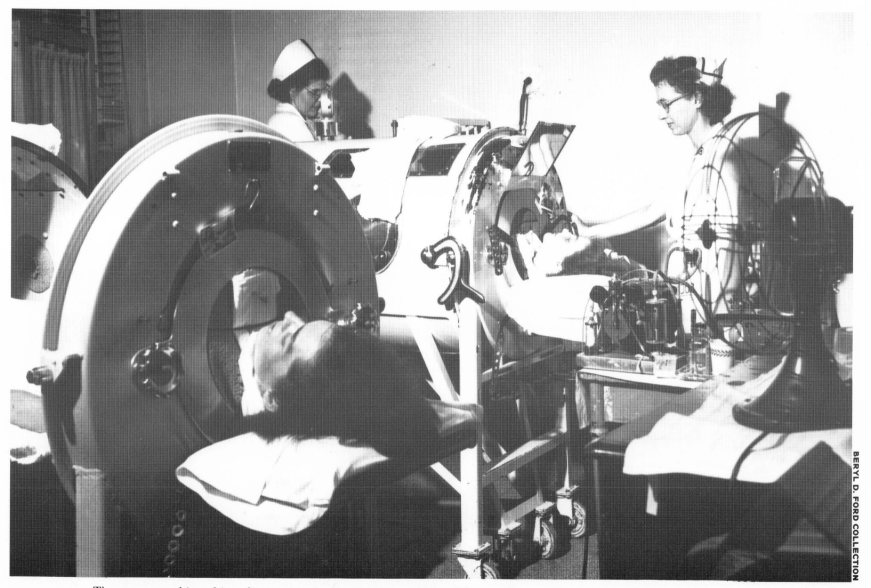

The constant whirr of iron lungs pumping oxygen into paralyzed lungs. The stench of wet wool from the hundreds of blanket strips soaked in scalding water and applied to aching limbs. These were the memories of nurses and parents long after the epidemic had ended.

130

Boy Scouts did the footwork for Tulsa's 1967 "Smash Polio" campaign. Tulsa's last reported polio case was in 1965.

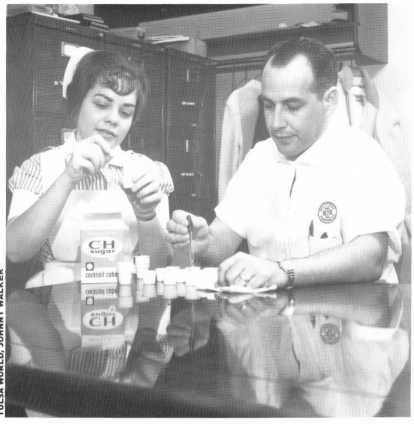

In 1955, the Salk vaccine conquered the disease that had killed or crippled 300,000 children. By 1967, an oral vaccine went down on a sugar cube.

Keep it clean was Tulsa's motto in 1955. A Chamber of Commerce "Beautification Campaign" had businessmen rolling out trash barrels and society matrons pushing a broom. In 1960, artful efforts by students boosted the clean-up effort.

Tulsa's Jewish Community Council gave global meaning to community spirit with a 1950 fundraiser for the fledgling state of Israel in the Mayo Hotel's Topaz Room. A year later, Abba Eban, then Israeli ambassador to the United Nations, visited Tulsa and was made an honorary member of Oklahoma's Otoe tribe.

133

Pavement emblazoned with skull and crossbones translated into "take care" to Tulsans in the mid-'50s when police marked the spot of traffic fatalities with the macabre motif.

A skirt's swish and a little leg, although admittedly hairy, were used to entice muggers when the Tulsa Police Department went undercover in the '50s.

All hands on duty: fire department electricians and other support personnel routinely were recruited for street duty when second alarms sounded and manpower was short. A second-string brigade toted a hose on North Main Street in the late '50s.

"Peace on Earth" was the winning theme in 1951 when Station 5, 18th Street and Boston Avenue, decked its walls with a Christmas mural.

137

The hula hoop: the coup de loop of the fabulous '50s.

THE WAY WE WERE

Tulsa came of age with a split personality.

To warm the inner man, fire-and-brimstone preachers competed with homemade hooch. The city bragged that it was a buckle on the Bible Belt, but thumbed its nose at Oklahoma's officially dry status. Tulsans flocked to tent revivals with Bible in hand — and a bootlegger's card in back pocket.

The '50s and '60s, in particular, profiled the city as an amalgam of the real and the imaginary, enduring values and adaptations, foresightedness and naivete.

Tulsa's proud handle, Oil Capital of the World, was by the '60s, and arguably much earlier, a misnomer. The spectacular discovery fields had moved on to new frontiers; so had big money. For most Tulsans, however, it didn't matter. The sobriquet lingered as a state of mind. "Tulsa," said one long-time industry observer, "was, and remained, the most oil-minded city ever."

Traditions of the boom years also endured. The city's wading pools, for example, were a '20s gift of oilman Frank Reed. For decades hence, opening day for this simple summer pleasure was a celebration. What's more, thousands of parents, lugging lawn chairs, still found time for lazy afternoons watching their offspring romp.

By the early '60s, the Health Department ruminated about the safety of the vintage watering holes. Tulsans, however, were chilled by a more contemporary threat, the escalation of the Cold War, the Cuban Missile crisis. Tulsa, they knew, was within range of the Russian-made missiles.

By then, "H-bomb," "radiation" and "Conelrad alert" already were household words. Ten staccato rings sent school children diving under their desks. By 1953, Tulsa had its first air-raid siren. A year later, the city participated in its first major civil-defense test which left a five-block section of Main Street deserted. Newspaper maps showed hypothetical bombing of Tulsa with ground zero at Fourth and Main streets.

Girl Scouts learned survival cooking. Emergency supplies were stockpiled in nearby mammoth caves. Advice abounded on the art of fallout-shelter living. "Build a $30 Fallout shelter," urged one newspaper article. "Reaching the shelter in time is only part of fallout survival," another went on. "Living in it the 14 days required for the fallout to become harmless is just as important."

By 1962, Tulsa was scouting out its most radiation-proof buildings for community air-raid shelter for 200,000.

Ultimately, it was all good for business, the fallout shelter business. By 1961, contractors had waiting lists. The shelter packages offered a variety of options including a specially electrified steel door to discourage unwelcome neighbors in event of atomic attack.

A '40s winter party of ice boaters and skaters on Lake Yahola, Tulsa's in-town reservoir.

When the summer sizzled in 1956, the ice was just as nice, even if man-made. The iceman's delivery at 10th Street and Boston Avenue provided an impromptu pause that refreshed.

Oilman Frank Reed began a Tulsa tradition in 1920 when he funded a chain of children's wading pools. The filling of the urban swimming holes meant that summer officially had begun. Weekly events such as catfish-catching contests drew hundreds of kids and their folks. The pools were closed in 1965 as a health hazard.

TULSA WORLD, JOHNNY WALKER

Summer of '59 champion wading-pool noodlers and their catch.

Sunbathing seemed top priority in 1960, but generations of Tulsans actually learned to swim at Newblock Park pool, the city's first — and for a long time sole — public pool. Early bathers, towel and swimsuit in hand, caught the Sand Springs interurban to take a dip. The pool, opened in 1929 on Charles Page Boulevard, was a recycled water department settlement hole. Ultimately, the city took a dim view of Newblock's origins. In September 1965, it was filled for the last time — with dirt for use as a parking lot.

143

The Corner Grocery and Market, 802 N. St. Louis Ave., was a neighborhood fixture by 1953. The Quik-Trip at 2238 E. 56th Place opened in 1965. Over a decade, the one-of-a-kind corner grocery, the original convenience store, gave grudging way to the proliferation of its streamlined progeny.

A Depression-era project, the Warehouse Market, 11th Street and Elgin Avenue, began as a farmers' market and became Oklahoma's largest volume supermarket. The Art Deco-style grocery still was drawing a parking lot full of shoppers in 1953.

145

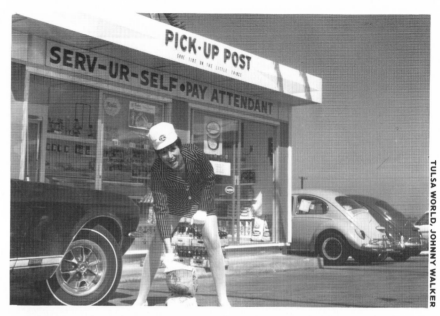

Above: By 1960, the automated milk machine was a common sight on Tulsa streets.

Above right: The skirts were mini; the service do-it-yourself in 1967 at the Pick-Up Post, another convenience-store prototype that marketed some of Tulsa's first pump-your-own gasoline.

Right: Not quite TransFund, but in 1957 Vend-a-Check let you "Take Five." The newest of vending machines, and Tulsa's first, was installed at the Warehouse Market, 11th Street and Elgin Avenue, and dispensed $5 checks.

Sixties suburbia: Saturday morning at the garage sale.

Before suburban malls, downtown was synonymous with shopping. In 1946, Oklahoma Tire & Supply Co., Second Street and Cincinnati Avenue, had it all from auto seat covers to "boy longies" for $1.29.

148

Shopping at the S.H. Kress 5-and-10, Third and Main streets, in 1956.

Back when a pack of cigarettes cost 20 cents, Old Golds were the center of attention for window-shoppers at Skaggs, Fifth and Main streets.

Skaggs was a Main Street fixture through the '50s.

In the '20s, Tulsa clinched its claim to the title "Oil Capital" by hosting the world's fair of the industry, the International Petroleum Exposition. Beginning with the 1953 IPE, nothing better symbolized that industry extravaganza than the Golden Driller, a giant papier-mache model of a bare-chested roughneck.

Left and far left: Popular demand brought back the Golden Driller — still papier-mache — for the 1959 IPE. *Below*: By 1966, a third-generation — and this time permanent — Driller was installed to guard the gates of the Exposition Building. Standing almost eight stories tall with 2½ miles of steel rod skeleton, he was one of the world's largest statues.

The world's then-best-known evangelist, Billy Graham, brought his old-time religion to Tulsa in June 1956 for a one-night stand that drew 28,000 to Skelly Stadium.

154

Sawhorses and cinder blocks constituted a humble platform for the tall, forceful preacher from North Carolina who had already carried his message to millions and called presidents by their first names.

In the '50s, Tulsa's own evangelist Oral Roberts drew thousands to a giant cathedral of canvas. He purchased his first "big tent" in 1948.

156

Ministering to the faithful in the '50s, the decade of the "healing tents."

For most travelling evangelists, the tents were modest; the pews, folding chairs on a dusty field floor.

ORAL ROBERTS EVANGELISTIC ASSOCIATION

TULSA WORLD, JOHNNY WALKER

157

Tales of Oral Roberts' miraculous faith healings drew standing-room crowds around the country.

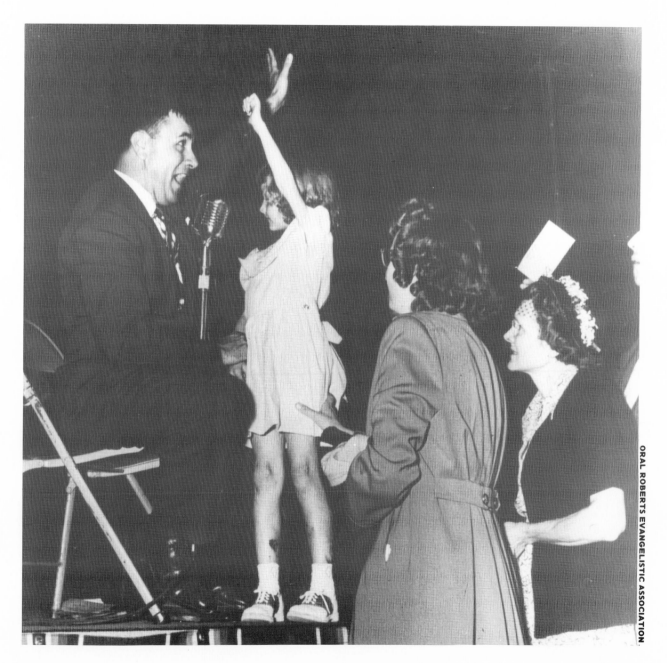

After a decade of ministering hands-on to his flock, Roberts, in a foreshadowing of his worldwide televangelism, took to the KRMG airwaves.

159

Tulsa felt the first chill of the Cold War in the mid-'50s. Construction of family fallout shelters, "starting as low as $150," was big business. Shelters contained special suits for testing for fallout.

160

Ready for war, while Tulsa school children took cover during an air raid drill, civil defense workers stored emergency supplies for Tulsa in mammoth caves near Fort Gibson.

In 1967, the mini on Main wasn't confined to m'lady.

Rosie the Riveter set the standard. By the mid-'50s, from the brokers' floor of Merrill Lynch to the assembly line of Zebco, women were in pants and on the job.

Mothers on the march in 1958 halted traffic to demand more school crossings and guards.

A postwar bread line at Ann's Bakery, 7 N. Harvard Ave., had nothing to do with shortages — except a shortage of workers. Employees of large bakeries that supplied grocery stores were on strike and Ann's family-baked loaves were at a premium.

University of Tulsa students marched against U.S. involvement in Vietnam.

In the early '70s, the "storm sewer people" gathered in a giant pipe at 41st Street for jam sessions.

Students and parents hoisted placards in 1960 to protest the planned closing of Benedictine Heights College, 21st Street and Lewis Avenue, then Oklahoma's only four-year Catholic college. The college received a temporary reprieve but shut down for good in 1966.

164

Signs of the times greeted Sen. Hubert H. Humphrey, Democratic candidate for vice president, in 1964 at Tulsa's Civic Center.

Oklahoma, courtesy of the 1907 state Constitution, was officially dry, but only in the law books. In Tulsa, bootleggers reigned, particularly in the '50s when a bottle of hooch was only a phone call away — and home delivery was expected. In 1957, a trunk-load of "lugs," three-packs of liquor, was confiscated by Tulsa police and never made it to the customer.

From a hole in the ground to a hollowed-out car door, bootleggers' hidey holes for hooch were paydirt for Tulsa police in 1957. Sometimes lawmen had to go to the source to dry up the flow of contraband whisky.

167

Liquor-to-go that
didn't.

Slot machines netted in
a 1957 Tulsa gambling
raid.

168

A gaming table saw its last dice roll.

169

Bootlegger business cards.

With liquor-by-the-wink, it was business as usual for many bootleggers to have lawmen in their pockets. In April 1957, the unholy alliance hit home when Tulsa's suspended Police Chief Paul Livingston, right, and Police Commissioner Jay L. Jones were convicted for plotting to break federal liquor laws.

A not-so-nostalgic landmark for some: Tulsa's old Municipal Court building, Fourth Street and Elgin Avenue, in 1956, also housed police headquarters and led the way to the no-frills city jail.

Inside the city jail in the '50s.

The emphasis was on "At last!" as Paul Walker Jr., a Tulsa repeal leader, watched a painter apply the final word to a window sign on April 7, 1959, the day Oklahomans voted "wet."

Oh Happy Day! Eager Tulsans in 1959 met the first legal truck load of liquor to roll over the state line, ending more than a half century of official dryness.

Born of Tulsa's boom days, the Metro Plaza Hotel went out with a bang in 1970.

COMING DOWN

Downtown needed a facelift.

As Tulsa pushed determinedly to fresh ground south and east, the business district where the city had planted its roots was reduced to a skid row.

Urban renewal was the answer. In the past, the wrecker's ball had swung frequently but selectively to clear the way for a bigger, better building, or sometimes a parking lot. But by the early '70s, whole blocks, once the city's premier real estate, were reduced to rubble. The way was cleared, planners said, for a revitalized downtown.

Demolition indeed vanquished the blight.

But the brick-and-mortar relics of Tulsa's pioneer past also were shattered.

Gone was Tulsa's first bank. Gone was the Grand Opera House. Gone was the Lynch Building. It was Tulsa's first masonry building, and downtown's oldest, surviving building. Also, it housed Tulsa's first formal theater, the Lyric.

But Tulsa wanted a shiny face.

The Lynch Building sagged. Grime smudged the storefront; the upper windows were nailed over with tin. Most of the doomed buildings were eyesores, but to Tulsans who cared to recall, the weathered facades spoke with mute eloquence of bygone eras, the heydays and the hurting times.

The Commercial Building, with a scant 25-foot frontage, was a white elephant of a modern office building, but when oil first gushed and young Tulsa boomed, it was a city pride, one of the first skyscrapers.

Only 20 years later, a nearby storefront was like commentary. It was the Depression and Uncle Willie's Donuts was a beacon to the hungry. A nickel bought a cup of coffee and two sinkers.

Urban renewal also claimed handsome skyscrapers in their prime. The Hunt Building with its decades-long tenant Brown-Dunkin was the ultimate evidence that downtown was the place to shop. But suburban centers challenged that distinction. By July 1970, the one-time undisputed paragon of shopping, was imploded.

It was a grand demise. For many other once-grand buildings, however, demolition simply was the final indignity.

The Grand Opera House, the original gathering place of Tulsa's elite, played out its last role as a cut-rate furniture auction house. The Lynch Building, its Lyric Theatre silent for almost 30 years, was a saggy roof over two pawn shops and a boarded-up tavern. The final curtain was hardly the star attraction of the summer of 1970. The two-story structure did not even rate a crowd-pleasing implosion. There was, however, an epilogue for the observant. When the two-foot thick walls of hand-cut stone finally crumbled, a bit of balcony and decorative fake windows clung to the adjoining building. It was guileless strip-tease, a final peak into a glamorous past for which there was no encore.

Urban renewal gave downtown Tulsa a facelift but stripped away pioneer heritage. Built in 1905, three landmark structures on the northeast corner of First and Main streets were among the casualties. The Archer Building, left, was named for one of Tulsa's founding families.

Tulsa's first masonry structure, the Lynch Building, southeast corner of First and Main streets, and the first bank, the Tulsa Banking Co., next door, also were razed. The Lynch Building, completed in 1894 with walls nearly two-feet thick, was believed to be downtown's oldest, still-standing building until its demolition in July 1970.

176

Dubbed an eyesore in the late '30s and Tulsa's No. 1 antique by the early '50s, Tulsa's stately County Courthouse, Sixth Street and Boulder Avenue, was vacated in 1955 when its successor became the first building completed in Tulsa's Civic Center.

Opened in 1912 with every convenience including a small gallows complete with gibbet, the courthouse, after being considered for a new central library, finally succumbed to the wrecker's ball in October 1960.

Remnants of records being removed before final demolition.

177

Second and Main streets in the '60s: once the heart of Tulsa's business district. The Commercial Building was one of the city's first skyscrapers.

Like a ghost of Tulsa's past, a faded vaudeville sign was all the evidence left in the '60s that the Lyric Theatre, First and Main streets, had been Tulsa's pioneer amusement center, "the pride of this end of Indian Territory." The playhouse was housed in the Lynch Building.

Closed for almost three decades, the Lyric Theatre revealed some of its glamorous past in July 1970 when demolition uncovered long-hidden walls, including decorative fake windows and the outlines of a balcony. The theater went dark in 1943 unable to compete with newer, fancier picture palaces.

179

The way it was: Main, north of Third Street in 1960.

The Bliss Building, constructed on the northwest corner of Third and Main streets in 1908, and neighboring S.H. Kress were demolished in 1974 to make way for the Williams Center "superblock."

Upper left: No longer so grand, Tulsa's Grand Opera House, 113 E. Second St., was built in 1906 — before the streets were paved — as a gathering place for the "elite." After spending its last five years as a furniture auction house, the curtain came down in 1966.

Above: It was the end of an era, the rocking chair era, when the Elks Lodge, southwest corner of Third Street and Boulder Avenue, was razed in 1957 for a parking lot. Dedicated in 1911 as the "jewel of Boulder Avenue," the lodge boasted a rocker-lined front porch where the Elks literally watched the city grow up around them.

Left: A gift from philanthopist Andrew Carnegie in 1915, Tulsa's Central Library building, Third Street and Cheyenne Avenue, was stately in design but woefully inadequate as the city grew. By 1956, 50,000 volumes had to be stored elsewhere, and the library was described as the worst in the nation for a city Tulsa's size. Remedy came in 1965 with the opening of the new Central Library.

Greenwood Avenue, the historic heart of North Tulsa, was another urban renewal target.

Opened in 1928, Wolferman's, 226 E. 15th St., was boom-town Tulsa's finest food store with much of its business done by telephone and delivery. The luxe, landmark grocery closed in November 1964 when a larger Wolferman's, that ultimately became Petty's Fine Foods, opened in Utica Square.

Temporarily a lone beacon in an urban renewal area cleared for construction of the Williams Center "superblock," the Metro Plaza Hotel, 123 S. Boston Ave., felt the wrecker's blast in February 1973. Built in 1929 as the Bliss Hotel, the 11-story hostelry's last years were spent as a roof to low-income elderly, many whose homes had been bulldozed by urban renewal.

183

184

Left: In transition: looking northeast at Third and Main streets in 1973, parking lots were the chief attraction of city blocks that once housed Tulsa's thriving pioneer business district. Soon, the blocks literally would rise again as the foundation for the Williams Center and Performing Arts Center.

Above: In 1959, the Drew Building, northwest corner of Third and Main streets, still had about a decade of life left in it. Tulsa Urban Renewal Authority purchased the Drew in 1968, completing acquistion for demolition of the block.

185

Going ... going ... gone. Eleven seconds was all it took in July 1970 to level the 11-story Medical Arts Building, built in 1929 at Sixth Street and Boulder Avenue. The demolition brought to four the number of landmark buildings that had been razed in a month period.

186

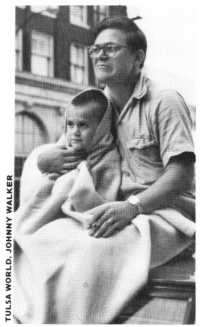

In 1950, Brown-Dunkin's 1,130 employees celebrated the company's 26th anniversary. Twenty years later, Tulsa's premier department store was closed when its home, the Hunt Building, was demolished to make way for the First National Bank's expanding complex.

The implosions of downtown's landmark buildings meant excitement for the young but a tumble of memories for their parents.

187

On the beam for the future, the Williams Center, keystone for a revitalized downtown, took shape in 1975 where the city had planted its roots almost 100 years before.

NEW DIRECTIONS

Tulsa had come full circle and was building on the ripples.

In 1882, pioneer merchants followed a trail of railroad spikes. They erected a tent city on vacant prairie acreage that would become Tulsa's premier business blocks, the prosperous promenade of oil barons.

Less than a century later, Tulsa focused again on its roots, dismayed. Rather than replace the historical, but mostly outdated structures, the city literally had moved next door, block by block, to erect its modern office buildings. The first downtown, that original core of commerce that centered at First and Main streets, was hopelessly decayed.

The answer was wholesale demolition. Urban renewal became the byword of the '60s. By the mid-'70s, Tulsa was ready to build again where it first had begun — this time the massive Williams Center complex. Almost simultaneously, the once-blighted blocks sported a bank tower, hotel, shopping forum and Performing Arts Center.

Reclaiming pioneer downtown was calculated renewal. It was Tulsa's innate prosperity, however, that pushed downtown, block by block from its origins, to build the bigger and the better. Those same ripples of prosperity also expanded the city's boundaries. By the '60s, waves of development were sweeping Tulsa south and east.

Once grassy crossroads were transformed into intersections weighted at each corner with a shopping center. By 1975, Woodland Hills Mall was rising at 71st Street and Memorial Drive. The intersection quickly was being widened — in anticipation of as much as four-million square feet of commercial space; a mini downtown in itself.

In 1976, the city got its newest tallest skyscraper, the 52-story Bank of Oklahoma tower of the Williams Center complex. It was a distinction that soon would be challenged — and, for the first time, not to another downtown building.

Evangelist Oral Roberts already had a world-wide following in 1962 when he became a South Tulsa pioneer breaking ground for his namesake university at 81st Street and Lewis Avenue. The futuristic campus was one of the greatest catalysts of growth for the area, and by 1981, Roberts had given his chosen neighborhood another distinction. He opened City of Faith Medical and Research Center. Its 60-story clinic topped the southeast Tulsa skyline.

The early '80s also added the peaks of the Mid-Continent Tower, Fourth Street and Boston Avenue, Warren Place complex, 61st Street and Yale Avenue, and the Kensington Galleria, 71st Street and Lewis Avenue. The city continued its push outward.

It produced a latter-day panorama that would have done a Tulsey Town pioneer proud. In less than a century, Tulsa had progressed from a lone beacon on the prairie to a string of urban pearls.

189

In the early '60s, Tulsa's skyline had the expansive look of success.

Building the long-awaited Civic Center: excavation was under way for the Tulsa City-County Library. It was completed in 1965. The County Courthouse, left, was the cornerstone of the complex, finished in 1954. The Convention Center, rear, opened in 1964. Still to come were the Municipal Courts Building and City Hall.

191

The completed Civic Center and a new 11th Street Bridge added new dimension to the 1972 cityscape.

The columned Corps of Engineers Building provided a vintage backdrop for Tulsa's changing profile, highlighted in 1975 by construction between Boulder and Cincinnati avenues of the Williams Center complex.

WIDE LOAD

The crumbled facades of urban renewal demolition were just memories in 1975 when the construction of the Williams Center and Performing Arts Center was in full swing. The 52-story Bank of Oklahoma, formerly National Bank of Tulsa, was about 10 percent complete with the work schedule calling for a floor a week.

In 1978, the Bank of Oklahoma Tower altered the Tulsa skyline.

In 1996, downtown Tulsa's skyline was
accented by the Inner Dispersal Loop.

There was much to attract Tulsans to downtown in 1996, such as the Mayfest celebration around the fountain at Bartlett Square.

Evangelist Oral Roberts paused for prayer March 2, 1962, at ground-breaking ceremonies for his name-sake university. By 1966, the futuristic campus which had sprouted in what was once a tomato field, was the taproot of Tulsa's spread southward.

By the early '80s, City of Faith crowned the expanding, internationally recognized center at 81st Street and Lewis Avenue.

Tulsa Junior College opened in a single building in downtown Tulsa in September 1970. As enrollment grew and its number of campuses swelled to four, the school changed its name in 1996 to Tulsa Community College. The Southeast Campus, above, is at 81st Street and U.S. 169.

Rogers University was created in 1996, the result of a merger of Rogers State College in Claremore and the University Center at Tulsa. The Tulsa campus, above, at 700 N. Greenwood Ave., is one of the school's four branches.

201

Memorial Drive, looking north at 71st Street, in the early '50s and in 1988.

Woodland Hills Mall, 71st Street and Memorial Drive, in 1982.

203

The 7.6-mile Creek Turnpike in South Tulsa was completed in 1992, linking U.S. 169 and the Mingo Valley Expressway with U.S. 75. The turnpike introduced Tulsans to toll booths and the latest in pay-as-you-go travel, the Pikepass.

Woodland Hills Mall, 71st Street and Memorial Drive, stood as Oklahoma's largest shopping center, with 1.2-million square feet of retail space, in 1997.

41st Street, looking east at Yale Avenue, in the late '50s and in 1988.

The 36-story Mid-Continent Tower, integrated with the 14-floor Mid-Continent Building, was completed in 1984. The original structure, Fourth Street and Boston Avenue, was built in 1916-18 by Josh Cosden. The tower, built by Reading & Bates Corp., was recognized by the National Trust for Historic Preservation for architectural-engineering innovation for its cantilever construction.

207

71st Street, looking west at Sheridan Road, in the early '60s and in 1988.

71st Street, looking west at Lewis Avenue, in the mid-'50s and in 1988.

210 "If we don't have the bridge, we don't need the roads, unless we put a ferry back there," said State Rep. Bob Hopkins, D-Tulsa, chairman of the house Roads and Highways Committee, during the decade-long push for a 71st Street bridge across the Arkansas River.

In 1983, the goal was realized with a new gateway to South Tulsa: the 71st Street Bridge.

As Riverside Drive stretched farther southward in the 1990s, the popularity of River Parks grew with it. Biking or walking, skating or jogging, Tulsans enjoyed an uninterrupted playground from 11th Street to 81st Street. And across the Arkansas River, on the west bank, the Reynolds Amphitheater provided a setting for the musical crowd.

Even as the century was beginning to fade away, Tulsa still was bridging the Arkansas River. Tulsa opened the century in 1904 with the first wagon bridge across the river at 11th Street. In 1996, eight miles south of that first bridge, Tulsa dedicated the 91st Street Bridge into Jenks.

213

214   Where it all began: First and Main streets, 1889.

Where we are today: less than 100 years later.

215

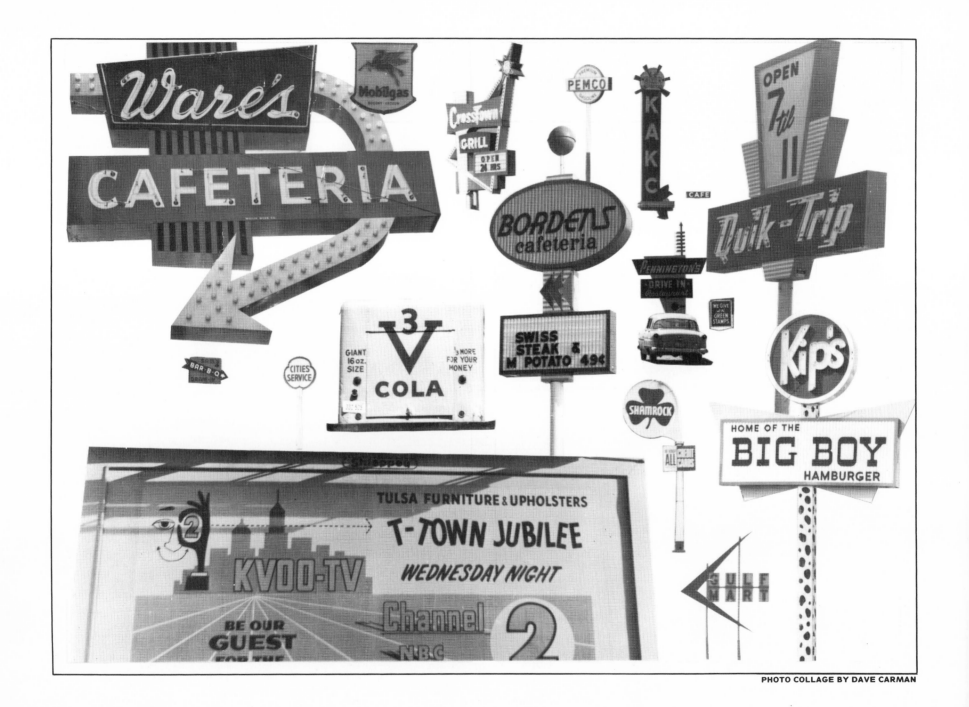

PHOTO COLLAGE BY DAVE CARMAN